BELOVED

This is YOUR year to create.
Make it an AMAZING year,
using your intuition and your
Tarot cards as a guide.

WELCOME

Welcome Beloved.

You are about to step into one of your most powerful years yet as you say YES to your intuition and your inner wisdom.

With your Tarot cards as a guide, you'll tune in to your Higher Self, manifest your goals and dreams and create a life that is in full alignment with your soul's purpose.

It's all possible with the Biddy Tarot Planner.

The Biddy Tarot Planner will give you the power to:

Tap into the collective energy of each month with the intuitive Tarot forecast

- Use monthly rituals to deepen your connection with the collective energy

- Reveal the opportunities, challenges and recommend actions for the month ahead, using your Tarot cards as a guide

- Set your new moon intentions and reflect on your full moon manifestations

- Plan your month of awesomeness, day by day

- Create personalised weekly forecasts to maximise your soul's energy

- Complete a juicy Tarot spread each month for the deepest intuitive insights into how make 2018 a wonderful year.

At the start of each Quarter, complete the Manifestation Tarot Spread to dream up your goals and discover how to turn your dreams into reality.

At the end of the Quarter, reflect on how far you've come with the Reflection Tarot Spread.

And throughout the year, dip into the monthly Tarot cards, rituals, new & full moon cycles to help you stay in full alignment with your Higher Self.

(Watch the free video tutorials on how to make the most of your Planner at www.biddytarot.com/planner-videos.)

So, get out your favourite Tarot deck, crystals, and markers and prepare to get 'up close and personal' with your intuition and inner wisdom.

This Planner has been designed for YOU, to help you create an amazing year ahead, with your intuition and Tarot cards as a guide.

Lots of love and success,

[signature]

P.S. If you're on Instagram, don't forget to share LOTS of photos of your Planner with #biddytarotplanner. I'd love to see what you create in 2018!

TABLE OF CON-TENTS

HOW TO MAKE THE MOST OUT OF YOUR PLANNER

To get started, here's what you will need:

- Your favourite Tarot deck. (Haven't got a deck yet? I recommend the Radiant Rider Waite deck available via www.biddytarot.com/radiant or the Lumina Tarot available via www.biddytarot.com/lumina)

- Your favourite markers, pens & pencils

- (Optional) Printed Tarot cards. At the back of the Planner, we've included images of the Rider Waite deck that you can copy and paste into your Tarot Planner as you do your Tarot readings.

Here's how you can make the most out of your Planner:

FIRST, WATCH THE VIDEO TUTORIALS...

I've created a series of tutorial videos to show you how to make the most of the Biddy Tarot Planner. I'll be there with you every step of the way!

For free access, go to www.biddytarot.com/planner-videos

In the meantime, here are a few tips to get you started...

AT THE START OF THE YEAR...

Start your year with the New Year Spread (on Page 10) – a divine experience of self-reflection, envisioning, and Tarot card consultation.

And connect with the energy of the 2018 Tarot card – Justice. Take some time to reflect on what its energy means for you as you step into the new year.

AT THE START OF THE QUARTER (JANUARY, APRIL, JULY & OCTOBER)...

At the start of each quarter, set your goals for the next 3 months, and then do the Manifestation Tarot Spread to discover how to bring your goals into fruition in full alignment with your soul's purpose.

Need some help setting intentional & intuitive goals? Make sure you watch my free video tutorial on how to create 'goals with soul' – access the videos at www.biddytarot.com/planner-videos

AT THE END OF THE QUARTER (MARCH, JUNE, SEPTEMBER & DECEMBER)...

At the end of the quarter, use the Reflection Tarot Spread to honour what you have manifested and learned along the way. This is perfect preparation as you move into the new quarter and begin to set new goals for yourself.

If you're on Instagram, I would love to see your Tarot spreads! Use the hashtag #biddytarotplanner to post your photos of the Planner and your readings, and we'll share them with the Biddy Tarot community!

AT THE START OF THE MONTH...

Reflect on the Tarot card for the month. I've shared some initial insights – take it to the next level by connecting in with what it means for you. How can you harness this energy and use it throughout the month ahead?

Next, do the ritual associated with the Tarot card. You may do the ritual just once during the month, or you may choose to do it more frequently. You can also continue to use the ritual in following months if you feel called to do so.

I've also recommended a crystal that you can work with to connect with the energy of the Tarot card. You could carry the crystal with you throughout the month, wear it, place it on your desk or in your bedroom, bring it out each time you do a Tarot reading – be creative!

Finally, I've included space for your very own weekly Tarot card forecast. At the start of the month, reflect on the month ahead, then draw a Tarot card for each week. The intention with the Weekly Tarot Card is not to predict 'what will happen', but more to help you connect into the energy of the weeks ahead and to make the most of that energy. Use it as a spiritual lesson or signpost, rather than a definitive prediction of the future.

ON THE NEW MOON & THE FULL MOON...

Inside the Planner, I've included the dates for the new moon and the full moon (check the dates for your specific time zone as they can be out by a day, depending where you live). Use these potent times to set your intentions and honour your achievements.

On the New Moon, set your intentions for the next 2 weeks and get ready to start new projects and make new beginnings. You might also be inspired to use the New Moon Manifestation Spread available via www.biddytarot.com/planner-videos. Then, as the moon waxes and becomes visibly larger, get to work and start manifesting your goals!

On the Full Moon, give thanks for what you have achieved and manifested over the past 2 weeks. Then as the moon wanes, prepare to descend into the darkness and let go what is no longer serving you, clearing and cleansing your energy and your space.

(Watch the free video tutorials for more ideas about how you can tap into the power of the lunar cycles – go to www.biddytarot.com/planner-videos.)

And while we're speaking about planetary influences, keep an eye out for Mercury Retrograde which occurs roughly 3 to 4 times per year. Mercury Retrograde is renowned for creating havoc with communication, timing, and technology. Avoid activities such as signing contracts, launching products, and making technical upgrades, and always double-check the details. That said, there are also positive aspects to Mercury Retrograde – it's the perfect time for reflection, revisiting the past, reworking or closing out a project, and re-evaluating your priorities (lots of 'RE's!!).

IF YOU NEED A LITTLE HELP WITH THE TAROT CARD MEANINGS...

To make the most out of the Biddy Tarot Planner, all you need is a basic knowledge of the Tarot cards and your intuition will take care of the rest!

However, I know for some of you may want a little extra guidance along the way so I have two options for you:

BOOK - THE ULTIMATE GUIDE TO TAROT CARD MEANINGS

This is my best-selling book with all of the meanings for the Tarot cards inside. Not only will you discover what the upright and reversed cards mean, you'll also learn how they translate in relationship, work, finance, spiritual, and well-being readings.

The best part? These aren't airy-fairy explanations of the cards – these are modern, practical and relatable so that you can quickly decipher the meaning of your Tarot readings. Buy the book at www.biddytarot.com/guide

ONLINE COURSE - MASTER THE TAROT CARD MEANINGS

 MASTER THE TAROT CARD MEANINGS

My program, Master the Tarot Card Meanings, is the #1 Tarot training online to help you instantly (and intuitively) interpret the 78 cards in the Tarot deck – without memorisation.

In Master the Tarot Card Meanings, I'll show you how to build a unique personal connection with the Tarot, using simple yet powerful techniques for interpreting the cards.

I'll teach you the 'must know' systems that sit behind the Tarot cards that make learning Tarot super simple.

And together, we'll walk through the 78 Tarot cards so you can master each and every one of them, once and for all!

Learn more at www.biddytarot.com/mtcm

REMEMBER...

- To make the most out of this Planner, check out my free video tutorials at www.biddytarot.com/planner-videos
- Post your photos of your Planner and Tarot spreads to Instagram with the hashtag #biddytarotplanner and we'll give you a shout-out!

2018 TAROT CARD - JUSTICE

The Tarot card for 2018 is the Justice card $(2 + 0 + 1 + 8 = 11 - Justice[1])$.

At its core, the energy of the Justice card is represented by:

- ⊚ Truth
- ⊚ Decision-making
- ⊚ Conscious awareness
- ⊚ Balancing the head and the heart

Throughout 2018, you will be called to examine your Truth. That is, what do you believe to be true? And how do you wish to express your Truth?

These may seem like simple questions on the surface, but once you begin to dig in and explore the depths of what your personal truth really is, you quickly realise that truth is not as black and white as it originally seems.

And this is the essence of the Justice card.

For example, you may believe murder to be wrong. But what about when you take a bite into your favourite hamburger and enjoy the juicy meat patty inside? (Don't worry – I'm also a meat lover!)

Or even if you're a peace-loving vegan (we love you!), do you still drive at sunset when there's a risk you might run into the mosquitoes and insects that love this time of night?

Where is the boundary? What is your truth? And what is ethically right or wrong?

It becomes murky and grey – but that's exactly what it's meant to be.

So, in 2018, be prepared to dip into those murky waters and explore what truth really means to you. Be consciously aware of what you believe to be true and what you believe to be fair and ethical. It may not be as clear-cut as you think, so be prepared to challenge yourself and to explore new territories of your belief system.

With the Justice card governing 2018, you will also become more aware of the decisions you make. Make decisions consciously this year. Don't be blind to the outcomes. Think things through with your eyes open wide. And be aware of the impact your decisions will have on your well-being and the well-being of others.

To be more consciously aware of your decisions, create a deep connection with your intuition. Every time you face an important decision or a cross-roads, tune in to your inner guidance system (AKA intuition) first and call for the answer.

---

[1] In the Rider-Waite deck, the 11th card of the Major Arcana is the Justice card. However, in other decks (including the featured Lumina Tarot), the 11th card is the Strength card, and Justice appears as the 8th card. Although the Lumina Tarot has Justice as the 8th card, I've chosen to work with the structure of the Rider Waite deck with Justice as the 11th card.

If you only think with your head or act impulsively, you will risk doing harm. But if you pause, tune in, and think with both your head and your heart, then you will find the answer that is most in alignment with your Higher Self.

You will also be called to account for the decision and choices you make, so be prepared to stand by your actions. At the end of the day, you need to be able to ask yourself, "Do I fundamentally stand by my decisions and accept the consequences of my actions?" If you cannot, then dig deeper, plunge into the shadows of what is right and wrong, until you find the place where you can stand in integrity and strength with the decisions you make.

Beloved, this is THE card for 2018, so come back to this page throughout the year and tune in to your connection with the Justice card. How can its energy help you and guide you during the course of the year? What lessons do you need to be reminded of, to live your fullest potential?

JOURNALING PROMPTS

Use these journaling prompts throughout the year to help you stay in alignment with the Justice energy.

1. WHAT IS MY TRUTH?

▷ INSIGHTS

2. HOW DO I KNOW THIS TO BE TRUE?

▷ INSIGHTS

3. WHAT ARE THE CONSEQUENCES OF MY DECISIONS?

▷ INSIGHTS

4. DO I STAND MY DECISIONS 100%?

▷ INSIGHTS

NEW YEAR SPREAD

THE PREVIOUS YEAR IN SUMMARY

LESSONS LEARNED FROM THE PAST YEAR

ASPIRATIONS FOR THE NEXT 12 MONTHS

WHAT EMPOWERS YOU IN REACHING YOUR ASPIRATIONS

WHAT MAY STAND IN THE WAY OF REACHING YOUR ASPIRATIONS

YOUR RELATIONSHIPS AND EMOTIONS IN THE COMING YEAR

YOUR CAREER, WORK AND FINANCES

YOUR HEALTH AND WELL-BEING

YOUR SPIRITUAL ENERGY AND INNER FULFILMENT

WHAT YOU MOST NEED TO FOCUS ON IN THE YEAR AHEAD

YOUR MOST IMPORTANT LESSON FOR THE COMING YEAR

OVERALL, WHERE ARE YOU HEADED IN THE NEXT 12 MONTHS

1. THE PREVIOUS YEAR IN SUMMARY

▷ CARD

▷ INSIGHTS

2. LESSONS LEARNED FROM THE PAST YEAR?

▷ CARD

▷ INSIGHTS

3. ASPIRATIONS FOR THE NEXT 12 MONTHS

▷ CARD

▷ INSIGHTS

4. WHAT EMPOWERS YOU IN REACHING YOUR ASPIRATIONS?

▷ CARD

▷ INSIGHTS

5. WHAT MAY STAND IN THE WAY OF REACHING YOUR ASPIRATIONS

▷ CARD

▷ INSIGHTS

6. YOUR RELATIONSHIPS AND EMOTIONS IN THE COMING YEAR

▷ CARD

▷ INSIGHTS

7. YOUR CAREER, WORK AND FINANCES

▷ CARD

▷ INSIGHTS

8. YOUR HEALTH AND WELL-BEING

▷ CARD

▷ INSIGHTS

9. YOUR SPIRITUAL ENERGY AND INNER FULFILMENT

▷ CARD

▷ INSIGHTS

10. WHAT YOU MOST NEED TO FOCUS ON IN THE YEAR AHEAD

▷ CARD

▷ INSIGHTS

11. YOUR MOST IMPORTANT LESSON FOR THE COMING YEAR

▷ CARD

▷ INSIGHTS

12. OVERALL, WHERE ARE YOU HEADED IN THE NEXT 12 MONTHS

▷ CARD

▷ INSIGHTS

EXTRA NOTES

Q1
2018

JAN | FEB | MAR

JANUARY

THE EMPEROR

The Emperor calls you to start the year with a plan – and the discipline to see it through. Set your intentional goals, then lay down the foundations and build the structure for your goals to come to fruition. Drop into the sacred masculine energy and take focused action this month to create the momentum you need to manifest your goals over the coming year. What you build now will determine your success later, so make sure the foundations are strong.

TAROT RITUAL

It's Action Planning time! First, pull the Emperor card from your deck and tune in to his masculine energy. Then, write down your goals for the year. What needs to happen for you to manifest these goals? What will guarantee success? Now, on a new piece of paper, draw four quadrants – one for each quarter of the year. Write in the actions you'll take in each quarter. You may need to move things around so you're not overloaded. Then ask yourself, What structure do I need in place to commit to these actions and manifest my goals?

CRYSTAL: JASPER

Supports organisational abilities, and imparts determination. Transform ideas into actions, and see your goals through until the end.

> ▷ INSIGHTS

REMINDER: January is the start of a new quarter, which means now is a great time to set your goals and do the Manifestation Tarot Spread.

SUN	MON	TUE	WED	THU	FRI	SAT
	● Full Moon 1	2	3	4	5	6
7	8	9	10	11	12	13
14	15	⚬ New Moon 16	17	18	19	20
21	22	23	24	25	26	27
28	29	30	● Full Moon 31			

⚬ NEW MOON INTENTIONS

1.

2.

3.

● FULL MOON ACHIEVEMENTS

1.

2.

3.

TAROT CARD OF THE WEEK

▷ CARD   ▷ INSIGHTS   ▷ ACTIONS

▷ CARD   ▷ INSIGHTS   ▷ ACTIONS

WEEK 3 | January 15 to 21

▷ CARD

▷ INSIGHTS

▷ ACTIONS

WEEK 4 | January 22 to 28

▷ CARD

▷ INSIGHTS

▷ ACTIONS

WEEK 5 | January 29 to February 4

▷ CARD

▷ INSIGHTS

▷ ACTIONS

MANIFESTATION SPREAD

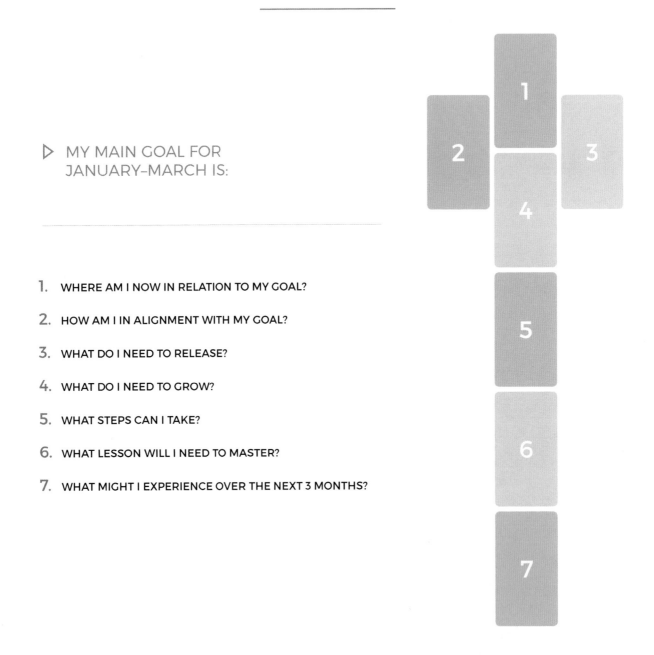

▷ MY MAIN GOAL FOR
JANUARY–MARCH IS:

_____

1. WHERE AM I NOW IN RELATION TO MY GOAL?

2. HOW AM I IN ALIGNMENT WITH MY GOAL?

3. WHAT DO I NEED TO RELEASE?

4. WHAT DO I NEED TO GROW?

5. WHAT STEPS CAN I TAKE?

6. WHAT LESSON WILL I NEED TO MASTER?

7. WHAT MIGHT I EXPERIENCE OVER THE NEXT 3 MONTHS?

NEED HELP WITH THIS SPREAD? Access my free video tutorials at biddytarot.com/planner-videos

1. WHERE AM I NOW IN RELATION TO MY GOAL?

▷ CARD

▷ INSIGHTS

2. HOW AM I IN ALIGNMENT WITH MY GOAL?

▷ CARD

▷ INSIGHTS

3. WHAT DO I NEED TO RELEASE?

▷ CARD

▷ INSIGHTS

4. WHAT DO I NEED TO GROW?

▷ CARD

▷ INSIGHTS

5. WHAT STEPS CAN I TAKE?

▷ CARD

▷ INSIGHTS

6. WHAT LESSON WILL I NEED TO MASTER?

▷ CARD

▷ INSIGHTS

7. WHAT MIGHT I EXPERIENCE OVER THE NEXT 3 MONTHS?

▷ CARD

▷ INSIGHTS

SUMMARY

EXTRA NOTES

FEBRUARY

THE FOOL

You have created the structures necessary for a successful year with the Emperor – now it's time to relax your grip and be 'in the flow' with the Fool. This card asks you to embrace your beautiful, carefree spirit, allowing yourself to feel into the energy of this month and how it flows through you. Tap into your fullest potential by stepping into a place of wonderment, curiosity and intrigue. Live life spontaneously, as if you were a child once again. Learn to laugh, to dance, to sing, to let your heart go free.

TAROT RITUAL

Take out the Fool from your favourite deck and tune into her energy. Now, put on your favourite music and dance as if no-one is watching. Close your eyes and let your body move in flow with the music. You might feel a little awkward at first – that's OK! Just keep dancing and keep letting go of all those niggling thoughts that get in the way of you being you. Let yourself be truly free and in flow.

CRYSTAL: DALMATIAN STONE

Tunes into your inner-child and stimulates playfulness and fun. Will help you to get out of your head and into your body to fully experience the world around you.

> ▷ INSIGHTS

SUN	MON	TUE	WED	THU	FRI	SAT
				1	2	3
4	5	6	7	8	9	10
11	12	13	14	◌ New Moon 15	16	17
18	19	20	21	22	23	24
25	26	27	28			

◌ NEW MOON INTENTIONS

1.

2.

3.

● FULL MOON ACHIEVEMENTS

NO FULL MOON
THIS MONTH

TAROT CARD OF THE WEEK

WEEK 6 | February 5 to 11

▷ CARD

▷ INSIGHTS

▷ ACTIONS

WEEK 7 | February 12 to 18

▷ CARD

▷ INSIGHTS

▷ ACTIONS

WEEK 8 | February 19 to 25

▷ CARD

▷ INSIGHTS

▷ ACTIONS

WEEK 9 | February 26 to March 4

▷ CARD

▷ INSIGHTS

▷ ACTIONS

SPIRITUAL COMPASS

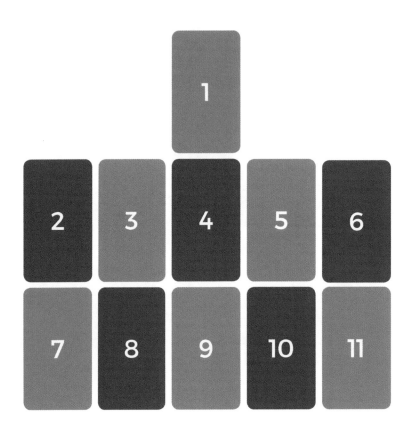

1. WHERE ARE YOU IN YOUR LIFE RIGHT NOW?

2. WHERE DO YOU WANT TO BE IN THE NEXT YEAR?

3. WHERE DO YOU WANT TO BE IN THE NEXT FIVE YEARS?

4. WHO ARE YOU BECOMING?

5. WHAT IS YOUR GREATEST TALENT OR POTENTIAL?

6. WHAT CAN YOU DO TO UNLOCK YOUR CREATIVITY?

7. HOW CAN YOU SPEAK YOUR 'TRUTH'?

8. WHAT CAN YOU DO TO CONTRIBUTE TO THE COMMUNITY?

9. HOW CAN YOU CONNECT WITH YOUR SACRED PATH?

10. HOW CAN YOU GET FROM HERE TO WHERE YOU WANT TO BE?

11. WHAT IS YOUR FIRST STEP?

ON INSTAGRAM? Post a photo of your spread and your Tarot Planner with the hashtag #biddytarotplanner and we'll share with the Biddy Tarot community!

1. WHERE ARE YOU IN YOUR LIFE RIGHT NOW?

▷ CARD

▷ INSIGHTS

2. WHERE DO YOU WANT TO BE IN THE NEXT YEAR?

▷ CARD

▷ INSIGHTS

3. WHERE DO YOU WANT TO BE IN THE NEXT FIVE YEARS?

▷ CARD

▷ INSIGHTS

4. WHO ARE YOU BECOMING?

▷ CARD

▷ INSIGHTS

5. WHAT IS YOUR GREATEST TALENT OR POTENTIAL?

▷ CARD

▷ INSIGHTS

6. WHAT CAN YOU DO TO UNLOCK YOUR CREATIVITY?

▷ CARD

▷ INSIGHTS

7. HOW CAN YOU SPEAK YOUR 'TRUTH'?

▷ CARD

▷ INSIGHTS

8. WHAT CAN YOU DO TO CONTRIBUTE TO THE COMMUNITY?

▷ CARD

▷ INSIGHTS

9. HOW CAN YOU CONNECT WITH YOUR SACRED PATH?

▷ CARD

▷ INSIGHTS

10. HOW CAN YOU GET FROM HERE TO WHERE YOU WANT TO BE?

▷ CARD

▷ INSIGHTS

11. WHAT IS YOUR FIRST STEP?

▷ CARD

▷ INSIGHTS

SUMMARY

MARCH

THE HANGED MAN

It's time to look at your world from a different perspective. Pause, step back and take some time away from your regular routine and schedule so that you can connect with a new way of thinking and seeing. Sure, you might have to literally put important projects on hold while you do this (and it might feel super inconvenient) but trust me, it'll be worth it. Something new is emerging and you won't be able to see it unless you allow the time and space for it to come through.

TAROT RITUAL

Find the Hanged Man in your favourite deck and drink in the imagery and energy for a moment. Then, take the morning or the afternoon off and do something you wouldn't normally do – go to a new park, a new beach, a new part of town. Hey, you might even be inspired to go to an acrobatics class or an aerial yoga class where you can literally hang upside-down. What new insights did you receive? What's your new perspective?

CRYSTAL: CHAROITE

A stone of transformation, Charoite stimulates positive vibrational movement by releasing the fears that may be holding you back from necessary change. It encourages perceptive observations and allows for new perspectives to enter consciousness.

> ▷ INSIGHTS

REMINDER: The end of March marks the end of the quarter. Now is a great time to use the reflection spread to honour what you have manifested and learned along the way.

SUN	MON	TUE	WED	THU	FRI	SAT
				● Full Moon 1	2	3
4	5	6	7	8	9	10
11	12	13	14	15	16 ⚬ New Moon	17
18	19	20	21 ☿℞	22 ☿℞	23 ☿℞	24
☿℞ 25	☿℞ 26	☿℞ 27	☿℞ 28	☿℞ 29	30	● Full Moon 31 ☿℞

☿℞ - Mercury Retrograde

⚬ NEW MOON INTENTIONS	● FULL MOON ACHIEVEMENTS
1.	1.
2.	2.
3.	3.

TAROT CARD OF THE WEEK

WEEK 10 | March 5 to 11

▷ CARD

▷ INSIGHTS

▷ ACTIONS

WEEK 11 | March 12 to 18

▷ CARD

▷ INSIGHTS

▷ ACTIONS

WEEK 12 | March 19 to 25

▷ CARD

▷ INSIGHTS

▷ ACTIONS

WEEK 13 | March 26 to Apr 1

▷ CARD

▷ INSIGHTS

▷ ACTIONS

REFLECTION SPREAD

1. WHAT WAS MY GREATEST 'WIN' THIS QUARTER?

2. WHAT LESSON DID I LEARN?

3. WHAT DO I NEED TO LEAVE BEHIND?

4. WHAT DO I NEED TO GROW AND NURTURE?

NEED HELP WITH THIS SPREAD? Access my free video tutorials at biddytarot.com/planner-videos

1. WHAT WAS MY GREATEST 'WIN' THIS QUARTER?

▷ CARD

▷ INSIGHTS

2. WHAT LESSON DID I LEARN?

▷ CARD

▷ INSIGHTS

3. WHAT DO I NEED TO LEAVE BEHIND?

▷ CARD

▷ INSIGHTS

4. WHAT DO I NEED TO GROW AND NURTURE?

▷ CARD

▷ INSIGHTS

EXTRA NOTES

Q2
2018

APR | MAY | JUN

APRIL

THE STAR

This month holds beauty, promise and inspiration for you. Right now, anything is possible and the magic is flowing around you. Your heart is filled with renewed hope and your soul is being uplifted to the highest of highs as you realise that your dreams really can come true. Allow yourself to dream, to aspire, to elevate in any way possible so that you can truly reach the stars. They are right here waiting for you.

TAROT RITUAL

In this month's ritual, you are invited to 'wish upon a star'. On the next starry night, take out the Star card from your favourite Tarot deck and connect with its energy. Then, go outside and look up into the stars and the universe above. Feel your heart and your mind expand into this infinite potential. Then, make a wish. Wish something that is so big, so dreamy, and so 'out there'. Hold your wish's energy in your heart, then hand it over to the Universe. The Universe has your back!

CRYSTAL: CLEAR QUARTZ

Clear Quartz – The universal stone. Quartz is the perfect stone for 'programming' your energy to manifest your desires, by raising your vibration to the highest level.

> ▷ INSIGHTS

REMINDER: April marks the start of a new quarter, which means now is a great time to set your goals and do the Manifestation Tarot Spread.

SUN	MON	TUE	WED	THU	FRI	SAT
☿ᴿ 1	☿ᴿ 2	☿ᴿ 3	☿ᴿ 4	☿ᴿ 5	☿ᴿ 6	☿ᴿ 7
☿ᴿ 8	☿ᴿ 9	☿ᴿ 10	☿ᴿ 11	☿ᴿ 12	☿ᴿ 13	☿ᴿ 14
○ New Moon 15 ☿ᴿ	16	17	18	19	20	21
22	23	24	25	26	27	28
● Full Moon 29	30					

☿ᴿ - Mercury Retrograde

○ NEW MOON INTENTIONS	● FULL MOON ACHIEVEMENTS
1.	1.
2.	2.
3.	3.

TAROT CARD OF
THE WEEK

WEEK 14 | April 2 to 8

▷ CARD

▷ INSIGHTS

▷ ACTIONS

WEEK 15 | April 9 to 15

▷ CARD

▷ INSIGHTS

▷ ACTIONS

WEEK 16 | April 16 to 22

▷ CARD

▷ INSIGHTS

▷ ACTIONS

WEEK 17 | April 23 to 29

▷ CARD

▷ INSIGHTS

▷ ACTIONS

WEEK 18 | April 30 to May 6

▷ CARD

▷ INSIGHTS

▷ ACTIONS

MANIFESTATION SPREAD

▷ MY MAIN GOAL FOR
APRIL-JUNE IS:

_____

1. WHERE AM I NOW IN RELATION TO MY GOAL?

2. HOW AM I IN ALIGNMENT WITH MY GOAL?

3. WHAT DO I NEED TO RELEASE?

4. WHAT DO I NEED TO GROW?

5. WHAT STEPS CAN I TAKE?

6. WHAT LESSON WILL I NEED TO MASTER?

7. WHAT MIGHT I EXPERIENCE OVER THE NEXT 3 MONTHS?

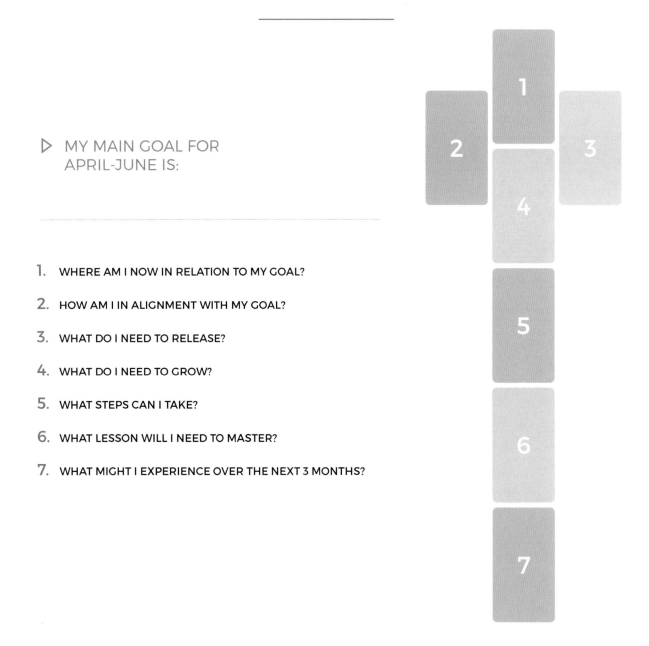

NEED HELP WITH THIS SPREAD? Access my free video tutorials at biddytarot.com/planner-videos

1. WHERE AM I NOW IN RELATION TO MY GOAL?

▷ CARD

▷ INSIGHTS

2. HOW AM I IN ALIGNMENT WITH MY GOAL?

▷ CARD

▷ INSIGHTS

3. WHAT DO I NEED TO RELEASE?

▷ CARD

▷ INSIGHTS

4. WHAT DO I NEED TO GROW?

▷ CARD

▷ INSIGHTS

5. WHAT STEPS CAN I TAKE?

▷ CARD

▷ INSIGHTS

6. WHAT LESSON WILL I NEED TO MASTER?

▷ CARD

▷ INSIGHTS

7. WHAT MIGHT I EXPERIENCE OVER THE NEXT 3 MONTHS?

▷ CARD

▷ INSIGHTS

SUMMARY

EXTRA NOTES

MAY

THE SUN

The Sun connects you to your power base – not fear-driven, egotistical power, but the abundant, inner power that is radiating through you right now. You'll feel it in your Solar Plexus chakra, calling you to express yourself fully and authentically, and be fully present in the world around you. You have what others want and you are being asked to radiate your energy and your gifts out into the world in a big way. Feel your personal power and use your Divine will to express that power in positive ways.

TAROT RITUAL

Find the Sun card in your favourite Tarot deck and connect with its energy. Then, find a place where you can meditate without interruption. Close your eyes, take a few deep breaths and ground yourself. Bring your attention to your Solar Plexus Chakra just above your belly button, and visualise a ball of warm, yellow light around this chakra. Imagine that yellow light filling your body, then radiating through your aura and out into the world. Experience the feelings of empowerment, Divine will, strength and abundance as you imagine this yellow light flowing through you and around you. And when you're ready, slowly open your eyes and come back into the room.

CRYSTAL: SUNSTONE

A joyful stone that restores your internal, positive energy and heightens intuition, so that you can nurture your personal power. It encourages optimism and a positive outlook.

> ▷ **INSIGHTS**

SUN	MON	TUE	WED	THU	FRI	SAT
		1	2	3	4	5
6	7	8	9	10	11	12
13	14	⚪ New Moon 15	16	17	18	19
20	21	22	23	24	25	26
27	28	● Full Moon 29	30	31		

⚪ NEW MOON INTENTIONS

1.

2.

3.

● FULL MOON ACHIEVEMENTS

1.

2.

3.

TAROT CARD OF THE WEEK

WEEK 19 | May 7 to 13

▷ CARD

▷ INSIGHTS

▷ ACTIONS

WEEK 20 | May 14 to 20

▷ CARD

▷ INSIGHTS

▷ ACTIONS

WEEK 21 | May 21 to 27

▷ CARD

▷ INSIGHTS

▷ ACTIONS

WEEK 22 | May 28 to June 3

▷ CARD

▷ INSIGHTS

▷ ACTIONS

THE CONFIDENT & INTUITIVE TAROT READER SPREAD

1. WHAT IS COMING INTO MY CONSCIOUS AWARENESS ABOUT READING TAROT?

2. WHAT INNATE GIFTS AND TALENTS DO I HAVE THAT I CAN SHARE WITH OTHERS IN MY TAROT READINGS?

3. WHAT ASPECTS OF MYSELF DO I NEED TO DEVELOP TO STEP INTO MY FULL POTENTIAL AS A TAROT READER?

4. WHAT ASPECTS OF MY TAROT READING SKILLS DO I NEED TO DEVELOP TO STEP INTO MY FULL POTENTIAL AS A TAROT READER?

5. WHAT EXTERNAL RESOURCES ARE AVAILABLE TO ME TO DEVELOP AS A TAROT READER?

6. HOW CAN I CONNECT WITH THE RIGHT PEOPLE WITH WHOM I WILL CREATE 'MAGIC' AS A TAROT READER?

7. WHAT IS POSSIBLE FOR ME WHEN I AM READING TAROT WITH CONFIDENCE?

ON INSTAGRAM? Post a photo of your spread and your Tarot Planner with the hashtag #biddytarotplanner and we'll share with the Biddy Tarot community!

1. WHAT IS COMING INTO MY CONSCIOUS AWARENESS ABOUT
   READING TAROT?

▷ CARD | ▷ INSIGHTS

2. WHAT INNATE GIFTS AND TALENTS DO I HAVE THAT I CAN SHARE
   WITH OTHERS IN MY TAROT READINGS?

▷ CARD | ▷ INSIGHTS

3. WHAT ASPECTS OF MYSELF DO I NEED TO DEVELOP TO STEP
   INTO MY FULL POTENTIAL AS A TAROT READER?

▷ CARD | ▷ INSIGHTS

4. WHAT ASPECTS OF MY TAROT READING SKILLS DO I NEED TO
   DEVELOP TO STEP INTO MY FULL POTENTIAL AS A TAROT READER?

▷ CARD | ▷ INSIGHTS

5. WHAT EXTERNAL RESOURCES ARE AVAILABLE TO ME TO
DEVELOP AS A TAROT READER?

▷ CARD | ▷ INSIGHTS

6. HOW CAN I CONNECT WITH THE RIGHT PEOPLE WITH WHOM
I WILL CREATE 'MAGIC' AS A TAROT READER?

▷ CARD | ▷ INSIGHTS

7. WHAT IS POSSIBLE FOR ME WHEN I AM READING TAROT
WITH CONFIDENCE?

▷ CARD | ▷ INSIGHTS

SUMMARY

EXTRA NOTES

JUNE

THE TOWER

Your world may start to crumble underneath you this month, in ways that are completely unexpected. What you thought was a solid structure has revealed itself as highly unstable and broken. The best way forward right now is to let this structure self-destruct so that you can re-build and re-focus. Change on this deep level is challenging, but you need to trust that life is happening FOR you, not TO you and this is all for a reason. You need this destruction so that new life can emerge and so that your soul can evolve in a powerful way.

TAROT RITUAL

On the new moon this month, light a black candle and turn the lights out. Pull the Tower card from your Tarot deck and take a moment to draw in its energy. What do you notice about the card? What feelings or thoughts does it stir up inside of you? Write this down in your journal. Then, blow out the candle and allow yourself to sit in complete darkness. Meditate on the structures in your life that may be crumbling right now. Visualise yourself tearing down these structures with intent and purpose, even if there is an initial resistance. And once the structures have been torn down, what emerges? What new growth is coming through? What is possible when you clear away the debris? When you are ready, open your eyes, turn on a dimmed light and write down your insights.

CRYSTAL: SMOKEY QUARTZ

Effective at grounding and anchoring, this stone will absorb any negative vibrations that surround you. In turn, it will raise your vibration and promote positive, clear thoughts while neutralizing fears.

▷ INSIGHTS

REMINDER: The end of June marks the end of the quarter. Now is a great time to use the reflection spread to honour what you have manifested and learned along the way.

SUN	MON	TUE	WED	THU	FRI	SAT
					1	2
3	4	5	6	7	8	9
10	11	12	New Moon 13	14	15	16
17	18	19	20	21	22	23
24	25	26	27 Full Moon 28	29	30

NEW MOON INTENTIONS

1.

2.

3.

FULL MOON ACHIEVEMENTS

1.

2.

3.

TAROT CARD OF THE WEEK

▷ CARD	▷ INSIGHTS	▷ ACTIONS

▷ CARD	▷ INSIGHTS	▷ ACTIONS

WEEK 25 | June 18 to 24

▷ CARD

▷ INSIGHTS

▷ ACTIONS

WEEK 26 | June 25 to July 1

▷ CARD

▷ INSIGHTS

▷ ACTIONS

REFLECTION
SPREAD

1. WHAT WAS MY GREATEST 'WIN' THIS QUARTER?

2. WHAT LESSON DID I LEARN?

3. WHAT DO I NEED TO LEAVE BEHIND?

4. WHAT DO I NEED TO GROW AND NURTURE?

NEED HELP WITH THIS SPREAD? Access my free video tutorials at biddytarot.com/planner-videos

1. WHAT WAS MY GREATEST 'WIN' THIS QUARTER?

▷ CARD

▷ INSIGHTS

2. WHAT LESSON DID I LEARN?

▷ CARD

▷ INSIGHTS

3. WHAT DO I NEED TO LEAVE BEHIND?

▷ CARD

▷ INSIGHTS

4. WHAT DO I NEED TO GROW AND NURTURE?

▷ CARD

▷ INSIGHTS

EXTRA NOTES

Q3
2018

JUL | AUG | SEP

JULY

JUDGEMENT

In the Lumina Tarot, Judgement is shown as a solar eclipse – a time of deep reflection, inner knowing and divine judgement, as you descend into darkness before returning to the light. This is incredibly potent as the Tower energy in June invited you to tear down the structures that are no longer serving you, and now the Judgement card in July is calling you to rise up and embrace a higher level of consciousness for the service of the Highest Good. Let go of your old self and step into this newest version of who you really are.

TAROT RITUAL

Take out the Judgement card from your favourite Tarot deck, look at the imagery and connect intuitively with its energy. Then, reflect on the following questions. What aspects of my Self am I letting go of? What new aspects of my Self are emerging? How can I be the best version of myself? Write your insights into your journal, using the Tarot cards to help you answer these questions and deepen your reflection. To end, light a sage smudge stick and wave the smoke over the back and front of your body to clear and cleanse your aura and to release any old or 'stuck' energy.

CRYSTAL: GREEN OR BLUE TOURMALINE

An excellent stone to help purify and cleanse heavy energies into lighter vibrations. Extremely beneficial in helping to understand ones' self by bringing mental processes and chakras into alignment.

> ▷ INSIGHTS

REMINDER: July marks the start of a new quarter, which means now is a great time to set your goals and do the Manifestation Tarot Spread.

SUN	MON	TUE	WED	THU	FRI	SAT
1	2	3	4	5	6	7
8	9	10	11 ☌ New Moon	12	13	14
15	16	17	18	19	20	21
22	23	24	25 ☿℞	26 ● Full Moon ☿℞	27 ☿℞	28
☿℞ 29	☿℞ 30	☿℞ 31				

☿℞ - Mercury Retrograde

◌ NEW MOON INTENTIONS	● FULL MOON ACHIEVEMENTS
1.	1.
2.	2.
3.	3.

TAROT CARD OF THE WEEK

▷ CARD

▷ INSIGHTS

▷ ACTIONS

▷ CARD

▷ INSIGHTS

▷ ACTIONS

WEEK 29 | July 16 to 22

▷ CARD

▷ INSIGHTS

▷ ACTIONS

WEEK 30 | July 23 to 29

▷ CARD

▷ INSIGHTS

▷ ACTIONS

WEEK 31 | July 30 to August 5

▷ CARD

▷ INSIGHTS

▷ ACTIONS

MANIFESTATION SPREAD

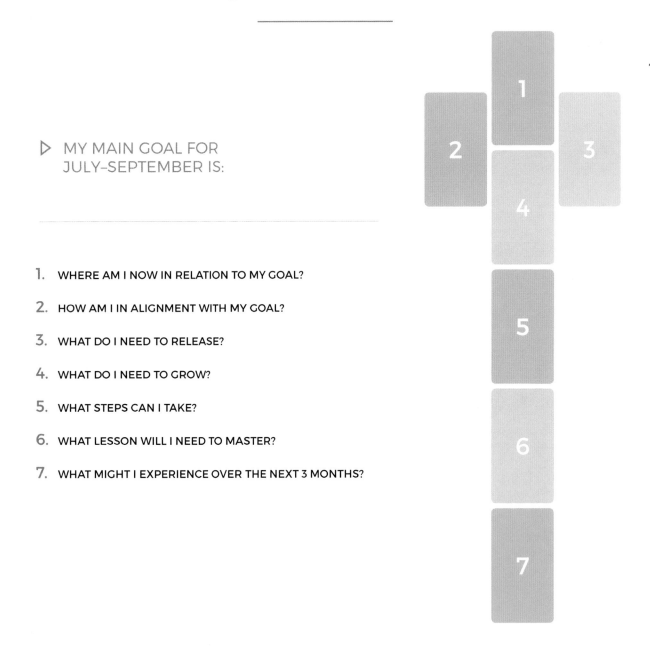

▷ MY MAIN GOAL FOR
   JULY–SEPTEMBER IS:

_____

1. WHERE AM I NOW IN RELATION TO MY GOAL?

2. HOW AM I IN ALIGNMENT WITH MY GOAL?

3. WHAT DO I NEED TO RELEASE?

4. WHAT DO I NEED TO GROW?

5. WHAT STEPS CAN I TAKE?

6. WHAT LESSON WILL I NEED TO MASTER?

7. WHAT MIGHT I EXPERIENCE OVER THE NEXT 3 MONTHS?

NEED HELP WITH THIS SPREAD? Access my free video tutorials at biddytarot.com/planner-videos

1. WHERE AM I NOW IN RELATION TO MY GOAL?

▷ CARD

▷ INSIGHTS

2. HOW AM I IN ALIGNMENT WITH MY GOAL?

▷ CARD

▷ INSIGHTS

3. WHAT DO I NEED TO RELEASE?

▷ CARD

▷ INSIGHTS

4. WHAT DO I NEED TO GROW?

▷ CARD

▷ INSIGHTS

AUGUST

TEMPERANCE

After an intense couple of months, the energy of the Temperance card brings you some welcome reprieve. You have successfully navigated the upheaval of the Tower and the upleveling of Judgement and can now return to a place of peace, calm and balance. You are being invited to balance and ground your energy this month, and to allow the life force to flow through you without force or resistance. It's time to find your flow once again and get your life back into order and balance.

TAROT RITUAL

First, find the Temperance card in your Tarot deck and connect with its energy. Then, go to your favourite place in nature where there is water – a creek, river, lake or beach. Stand in the water and feel it flowing gently over your feet. Ground yourself through the sand, rocks or pebbles underneath. Then tilt your face to the sky and feel the warmth of the sun on your skin. Connect to the Universal energy and feel it flowing down through you, in perfect balance and harmony.

CRYSTAL: ARAGONITE

A healing/grounding stone that is attuned to the Earth Goddess, aragonite stabilizes the root chakra. Useful in times of stress, it will help you to find your balance.

> ▷ INSIGHTS

SUN	MON	TUE	WED	THU	FRI	SAT
			☿℞ 1	☿℞ 2	☿℞ 3	☿℞ 4
☿℞ 5	☿℞ 6	☿℞ 7	☿℞ 8	☿℞ 9	☿℞ 10	○ New Moon 11 ☿℞
☿℞ 12	☿℞ 13	☿℞ 14	☿℞ 15	☿℞ 16	☿℞ 17	☿℞ 18
19	20	21	22	23	24	25
● Full Moon 26	27	28	29	30	31	

☿℞ - Mercury Retrograde

☼ NEW MOON INTENTIONS

1.

2.

3.

● FULL MOON ACHIEVEMENTS

1.

2.

3.

TAROT CARD OF THE WEEK

▷ CARD

▷ INSIGHTS

▷ ACTIONS

▷ CARD

▷ INSIGHTS

▷ ACTIONS

WEEK 34 | August 20 to 26

▷ CARD

▷ INSIGHTS

▷ ACTIONS

WEEK 35 | August 27 to September 2

▷ CARD

▷ INSIGHTS

▷ ACTIONS

HORSESHOE
SPREAD

1. PAST

2. PRESENT

3. NEAR FUTURE

4. SURROUNDING ENERGIES

5. ATTITUDE

6. OUTCOME

7. THE ANSWER

ON INSTAGRAM? Post a photo of your spread and your Tarot Planner with the hashtag #biddytarotplanner and we'll share with the Biddy Tarot community!

1. PAST

▷ CARD

▷ INSIGHTS

2. PRESENT

▷ CARD

▷ INSIGHTS

3. NEAR FUTURE

▷ CARD

▷ INSIGHTS

4. SURROUNDING ENERGIES

▷ CARD

▷ INSIGHTS

5. ATTITUDE

▷ CARD

▷ INSIGHTS

6. OUTCOME

▷ CARD

▷ INSIGHTS

7. THE ANSWER

▷ CARD

▷ INSIGHTS

SUMMARY

EXTRA NOTES

SEPTEMBER

THE LOVERS

September is the month for conscious connections and meaningful relationships. At the heart of it, the Lovers is about choice. Choice about who you spend time with. Choice about who you let into your life. Choice about how you interact with others and on what level. What are you choosing this month, when it comes to your relationships? Be mindful about your interactions with others and invest your energy with those who truly light you up or raise your vibration. And be open to exploring both the light and dark aspects of your relationships with others, taking the good with the bad and making conscious connections.

TAROT RITUAL

Take out the Lovers card from your Tarot deck and reflect on its energy. Then, find a quiet place and light a candle and burn some rose or ylang ylang oil. Close your eyes and connect with your heart chakra. Visualise a ball of pink light radiating from your heart centre. Feel this light growing and growing as it fills your body, then radiates out from you into your aura, your room, your neighbourhood, and eventually into the world and universe. Take a moment to feel this deep, radiant love. And say this affirmation 3 times – "I honour the love inside me and connect consciously with others." When you're ready, open your eyes and journal your experience.

CRYSTAL: ROSE QUARTZ

The stone of peace and unconditional love ... it is effective is drawing in those loving relationships and deflecting negative energies. Rose Quartz will help you open your heart to love and beauty by healing unexpressed heartaches and transmuting internalized pains that no longer serve you.

▷ INSIGHTS

REMINDER: The end of September marks the end of the quarter. Now is a great time to use the reflection spread to honour what you have manifested and learned along the way.

SUN	MON	TUE	WED	THU	FRI	SAT
						1
2	3	4	5	6	7	8
☼ New Moon 9	10	11	12	13	14	15
16	17	18	19	20	21	22
23	● Full Moon 24	25	26	27	28	29
30						

1.

2.

3.

● FULL MOON ACHIEVEMENTS

1.

2.

3.

TAROT CARD OF
THE WEEK

WEEK 36 | September 3 to 9

▷ CARD

▷ INSIGHTS

▷ ACTIONS

WEEK 37 | September 10 to 16

▷ CARD

▷ INSIGHTS

▷ ACTIONS

WEEK 38 | September 17 to 23

▷ CARD

▷ INSIGHTS

▷ ACTIONS

WEEK 39 | September 24 to 30

▷ CARD

▷ INSIGHTS

▷ ACTIONS

REFLECTION
SPREAD

1. WHAT WAS MY GREATEST 'WIN' THIS QUARTER?

2. WHAT LESSON DID I LEARN?

3. WHAT DO I NEED TO LEAVE BEHIND?

4. WHAT DO I NEED TO GROW AND NURTURE?

NEED HELP WITH THIS SPREAD? Access my free video tutorials at biddytarot.com/planner-videos

1. WHAT WAS MY GREATEST 'WIN' THIS QUARTER?

▷ CARD

▷ INSIGHTS

2. WHAT LESSON DID I LEARN?

▷ CARD

▷ INSIGHTS

3. WHAT DO I NEED TO LEAVE BEHIND?

▷ CARD

▷ INSIGHTS

4. WHAT DO I NEED TO GROW AND NURTURE?

▷ CARD

▷ INSIGHTS

EXTRA NOTES

Q4
2018

OCT | NOV | DEC

OCTOBER

THE MOON

This month, pay close attention to the moon cycles and attune with its divine power with a New and Full Moon ritual (see below). Connect with the divine feminine and uncover deep intuitive insights and visions of what lies beyond everyday life. The time is ripe to illuminate what is lurking in the shadows and what needs to be released, so that new aspects of yourself can shine through. Feel into situations, rather than thinking, especially as not everything is what it seems this month. Your intuitive abilities are dialled in right now, so use them to suss out what's really happening beneath the surface.

TAROT RITUAL

On the New Moon (October 8), set your intentions for the next 2 weeks and get ready to start new projects and make new beginnings. Then, as the moon waxes, get to work and start creating! On the Full Moon (October 24), give thanks for what you have achieved and manifested over the past 2 weeks. Then as the moon wanes, prepare to descend into the darkness and let go what is no longer serving you, clearing and cleansing your energy and your space.

CRYSTAL: MOONSTONE

As the stone of new beginnings, moonstone is perfect to support those new-moon intentions. It helps to promote intuition and clarity, and will help bring those unconscious thoughts, into consciousness.

▷ INSIGHTS

REMINDER: October marks the start of a new quarter, which means now is a great time to set your goals and do the Manifestation Tarot Spread.

SUN	MON	TUE	WED	THU	FRI	SAT
	1	2	3	4	5	6
7	⬡ New Moon 8	9	10	11	12	13
14	15	16	17	18	19	20
21	22	23	● Full Moon 24	25	26	27
28	29	30	31			

⬡ NEW MOON INTENTIONS	● FULL MOON ACHIEVEMENTS
1.	1.
2.	2.
3.	3.

TAROT CARD OF THE WEEK

WEEK 40 | October 1 to 7

▷ CARD

▷ INSIGHTS

▷ ACTIONS

WEEK 41 | October 8 to 14

▷ CARD

▷ INSIGHTS

▷ ACTIONS

WEEK 42 | October 15 to 21

▷ CARD

▷ INSIGHTS

▷ ACTIONS

WEEK 43 | October 22 to 28

▷ CARD

▷ INSIGHTS

▷ ACTIONS

WEEK 44 | October 29 to November 4

▷ CARD

▷ INSIGHTS

▷ ACTIONS

MANIFESTATION SPREAD

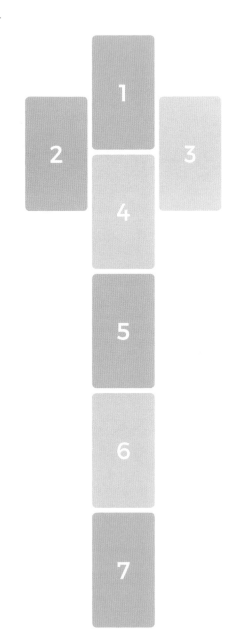

▷ MY MAIN GOAL FOR
OCTOBER–DECEMBER IS:

1. WHERE AM I NOW IN RELATION TO MY GOAL?

2. HOW AM I IN ALIGNMENT WITH MY GOAL?

3. WHAT DO I NEED TO RELEASE?

4. WHAT DO I NEED TO GROW?

5. WHAT STEPS CAN I TAKE?

6. WHAT LESSON WILL I NEED TO MASTER?

7. WHAT MIGHT I EXPERIENCE OVER THE NEXT 3 MONTHS?

NEED HELP WITH THIS SPREAD? Access my free video tutorials at biddytarot.com/planner-videos

1. WHERE AM I NOW IN RELATION TO MY GOAL?

▷ CARD

▷ INSIGHTS

2. HOW AM I IN ALIGNMENT WITH MY GOAL?

▷ CARD

▷ INSIGHTS

3. WHAT DO I NEED TO RELEASE?

▷ CARD

▷ INSIGHTS

4. WHAT DO I NEED TO GROW?

▷ CARD

▷ INSIGHTS

5. WHAT STEPS CAN I TAKE?

▷ CARD

▷ INSIGHTS

6. WHAT LESSON WILL I NEED TO MASTER?

▷ CARD

▷ INSIGHTS

7. WHAT MIGHT I EXPERIENCE OVER THE NEXT 3 MONTHS?

▷ CARD

▷ INSIGHTS

SUMMARY

NOVEMBER

THE WORLD

As the year comes to an end, you are feeling a sense of wholeness and completion. All the triumphs and tribulations have come full circle and you can now sit in this beautiful place of being able to reflect on the past 11 months, honouring your achievements and tuning into your spiritual lessons. This is the perfect time to express gratitude for what you have created and harvested this year. And it is also time to now close out this year's key projects, in preparation for the new year of 2019.

TAROT RITUAL

Take out the World card from your Tarot deck and place it in front of you, drawing in its energy. Light a candle and say out loud, "I open this sacred space and give thanks for all that I have experienced this year." Now, reflect on your achievements and experiences of the past 11 months and write them down in your journal. Don't just limit yourself to the successes – also reflect on the challenging moments of this year and the opportunities that emerged from those challenges. Now, reflect on what you have learned from the year and write these lessons down. Finally, reflect on how you can bring a sense of closure and completion to this year. To end the ritual, blow out the candle, saying out loud, "I close this sacred space and give thanks for all that I have experienced this year."

CRYSTAL: AMETHYST

A high-vibrational, protective stone; Amethyst balances out the highs and lows of life, bringing peace and understanding. It helps you to remain focused and appreciative of all the blessings around you.

▷ INSIGHTS

SUN	MON	TUE	WED	THU	FRI	SAT
				1	2	3
4	5	6	☼ New Moon 7	8	9	10
11	12	13	14	15	☿℞ 16	☿℞ 17
☿℞ 18	☿℞ 19	☿℞ 20	☿℞ 21	☿℞ 22	☿℞ 23	☿℞ 24
☿℞ 25	☿℞ 26	● Full Moon 27 ☿℞	☿℞ 28	☿℞ 29	☿℞ 30	

☿℞ - Mercury Retrograde

☼ NEW MOON INTENTIONS

1.

2.

3.

● FULL MOON ACHIEVEMENTS

1.

2.

3.

TAROT CARD OF THE WEEK

WEEK 45 | November 5 to 11

▷ CARD	▷ INSIGHTS	▷ ACTIONS

WEEK 46 | November 12 to 18

▷ CARD	▷ INSIGHTS	▷ ACTIONS

WEEK 47 | November 19 to 25

▷ CARD

▷ INSIGHTS

▷ ACTIONS

WEEK 48 | November 26 to December 2

▷ CARD

▷ INSIGHTS

▷ ACTIONS

THE CHAKRA SPREAD

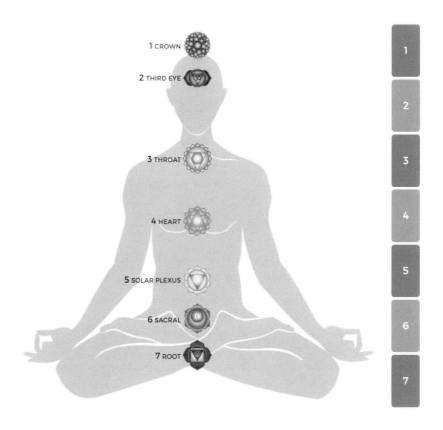

1. WHAT IS MY DIVINE CALLING?

2. HOW CAN I CONNECT WITH MY INNER WISDOM?

3. HOW CAN I SPEAK MY 'TRUTH'?

4. HOW CAN I EXPRESS LOVE?

5. WHAT EMPOWERS ME?

6. HOW CAN I EXPRESS MY CREATIVITY?

7. WHAT GROUNDS ME?

ON INSTAGRAM? Post a photo of your spread and your Tarot Planner with the hashtag #biddytarotplanner and we'll share with the Biddy Tarot community!

1. WHAT IS MY DIVINE CALLING?

▷ CARD

▷ INSIGHTS

2. HOW CAN I CONNECT WITH MY INNER WISDOM?

▷ CARD

▷ INSIGHTS

3. HOW CAN I SPEAK MY 'TRUTH'?

▷ CARD

▷ INSIGHTS

4. HOW CAN I EXPRESS LOVE?

▷ CARD

▷ INSIGHTS

5. WHAT EMPOWERS ME?

▷ CARD

▷ INSIGHTS

6. HOW CAN I EXPRESS MY CREATIVITY?

▷ CARD

▷ INSIGHTS

7. WHAT GROUNDS ME?

▷ CARD

▷ INSIGHTS

SUMMARY

EXTRA NOTES

DECEMBER

DEATH

The World in November was a gentle reminder to bring closure to key aspects of your life. Now, with the Death card in December, you are being called to make this closure more 'final'. What aspects of your life are going through a metaphorical death right now? What can you let go and leave behind? It may feel uncomfortable to be so final and the resistance may rise up, but remind yourself that with death, there is life, and with life, there is death. By letting go, what are you allowing to emerge and grow? What transformation can you create?

TAROT RITUAL

This is an intense ritual, perhaps too intense for some, but also a very powerful ritual – so please do this ritual mindfully. Take out the Death card and light a candle. Meditate on the concept of death and transformation. Then when you are ready, bring your attention inwards and connect with your inner source of energy. Imagine that today is the last day of your life. You are stripped of your past and your identity, and all that is left is your pure source energy. You may even imagine yourself dying, melting into the ground, fading away. Then, imagine yourself being reborn and recreated, from that pure source of energy. Experience a sense of peace and deep truth as you step fully into this transformation. You are refreshed and revitalised. And when you are ready, come back into the room and journal your experience.

CRYSTAL: CARNELIAN

Known to help instil acceptance of 'the cycle of life', it is useful in grounding you to present reality, helping to distinguish what no longer serves you by learning to trust yourself and your perceptions. This high energy stone stimulates courage and helps to overcome negative conditioning that has been learned over time.

▷ INSIGHTS

REMINDER: The end of December not only marks the end of the quarter, but also the year. Now is a great time to use the reflection spread to honour what you have manifested and learned along the way.

SUN	MON	TUE	WED	THU	FRI	SAT
					☿ᴿ	1
☿ᴿ 2	☿ᴿ 3	☿ᴿ 4	☿ᴿ 5	☿ᴿ 6	◌ New Moon 7	8
9	10	11	12	13	14	15
16	17	18	19	20	21	● Full Moon 22
23	24	25	26	27	28	29
30	31					

◌ NEW MOON INTENTIONS	● FULL MOON ACHIEVEMENTS
1.	1.
2.	2.
3.	3.

TAROT CARD OF THE WEEK

▷ CARD

▷ INSIGHTS

▷ ACTIONS

▷ CARD

▷ INSIGHTS

▷ ACTIONS

WEEK 51 | December 17 to 23

▷ CARD

▷ INSIGHTS

▷ ACTIONS

WEEK 52 | December 24 to 31

▷ CARD

▷ INSIGHTS

▷ ACTIONS

HOLIDAY SPREAD

1. WHAT IS YOUR 'STAR' (YOUR BLESSING) THAT SHINES BRIGHTLY?

2. WHAT GIFT DOES THE UNIVERSE HAVE FOR YOU?

3. WHAT GIFT CAN YOU SHARE WITH THE WORLD?

4. WHAT GIFT CAN YOU SHARE WITH YOURSELF?

5. WHAT NEW LIFE IS BEING BORN IN YOUR WORLD?

6. WHAT GIVES YOU RENEWED HOPE AND FAITH AS YOU ENTER THE NEW YEAR?

7. HOW CAN YOU SPREAD THE LOVE WITH YOUR LOVED ONES?

ON INSTAGRAM? Post a photo of your spread and your Tarot Planner with the hashtag #biddytarotplanner and we'll share with the Biddy Tarot community!

1. WHAT IS YOUR 'STAR' (YOUR BLESSING) THAT SHINES BRIGHTLY?

▷ CARD

▷ INSIGHTS

2. WHAT GIFT DOES THE UNIVERSE HAVE FOR YOU?

▷ CARD

▷ INSIGHTS

3. WHAT GIFT CAN YOU SHARE WITH THE WORLD?

▷ CARD

▷ INSIGHTS

4. WHAT GIFT CAN YOU SHARE WITH YOURSELF?

▷ CARD

▷ INSIGHTS

5. WHAT NEW LIFE IS BEING BORN IN YOUR WORLD?

▷ CARD

▷ INSIGHTS

6. WHAT GIVES YOU RENEWED HOPE AND FAITH AS YOU ENTER THE NEW YEAR?

▷ CARD

▷ INSIGHTS

7. HOW CAN YOU SPREAD THE LOVE WITH YOUR LOVED ONES?

▷ CARD

▷ INSIGHTS

SUMMARY

PRINT-YOUR-OWN TAROT CARDS

THE FOOL.   THE MAGICIAN.   THE HIGH PRIESTESS.   THE EMPRESS.   THE EMPEROR.   THE HIEROPHANT.   THE LOVERS.

THE CHARIOT.   STRENGTH.   THE HERMIT.   WHEEL of FORTUNE.   JUSTICE.   THE HANGED MAN.   DEATH.

TEMPERANCE.   THE DEVIL.   THE TOWER.   THE STAR.   THE MOON.   THE SUN.   JUDGEMENT.

THE WORLD.   KING of WANDS.   QUEEN of WANDS.   KNIGHT of WANDS.   PAGE of WANDS.

PAGE INTENTIONALLY LEFT BLANK

PRINT-YOUR-OWN
TAROT CARDS

[CONT'D]

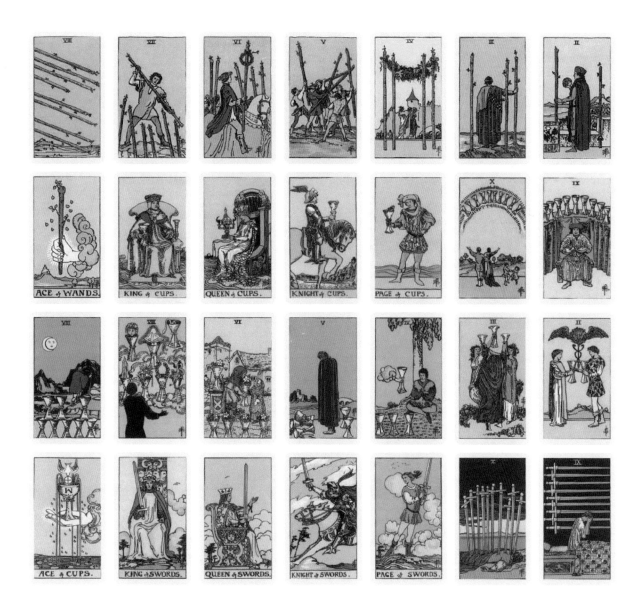

PAGE INTENTIONALLY LEFT BLANK

PRINT-YOUR-OWN
TAROT CARDS

[CONT'D]

Made in the USA
Columbia, SC
17 January 2018